STEAM MEMORIES: 1950's – 1960's

No. 33: CARLISLE

Including: *Carlisle Citadel Station, Kingmoor, Upperby & Canal locomotive sheds*

Copyright Book Law Publications 2009
ISBN 978-1-907094-54-5

INTRODUCTION

My first visit to Carlisle was in the summer of 1956, at that time I was still a young schoolboy. Travelling behind V3 67653 of Blaydon with a couple of older friends I was to be introduced to the joys of the London Midland and Scottish Railway and also instructed in the art of shed 'Bunking'. Being brought up on Gresley Pacifics and pre-grouping North Eastern locomotives this was a whole new world to me. Alighting the train in Carlisle Citadel station, I was to be amazed by the variety of engines I would see, Stanier, Ivatt, Fowler, Fairburn, Hughes, McIntosh and also Riddles standard designs; as a boy I had not realised the railway history of this place called Carlisle!

Carlisle has always been a Mecca for railway enthusiasts, from pre-grouping days right through to almost the end of steam on British Railways. Prior to the grouping, no less than seven railway companies worked into Citadel station, The London North Western, Midland and Maryport and Carlisle from the south, The North Eastern from the east and The Caledonian, Glasgow South Western and The North British from the north, each with its own selection of locomotives and their distinctive liveries. After the grouping and even after nationalisation, the variety of locomotive classes to be seen in the Border City was amongst the highest on the railway network, with many pre-grouping designs still in service.

The engine sheds serving the city in 1956 were Upperby, Kingmoor, Canal and Durran Hill. Upperby, the LNWR shed serving north and south had many passenger turns, and consequently had an allocation of over one hundred engines including Patriots, Jubilees, Royal Scots and Coronations, all those lovely namer's. The Caledonian shed Kingmoor, served the north and west with an allocation of nearly one hundred and fifty, mainly Crabs, Black fives, Jubilees and five Clans for use on The Port Road to Stranraer. The NB shed Canal with the smallest allocation of sixty, served Newcastle, Silloth and Edinburgh (The Waverley Route), of course here we have the Gresley A3s Sir Visto, Bayardo, Coronach and Flamingo which were rarely seen south of Newcastle, and a selection of ex NB classes D31, J35, J36, C15 and N15 supplemented with D49 Shire and B1s. Durran Hill the Midland shed, which had closed in the thirties, had no allocation but was used as a stabling point, and an extremely long walk from the city centre, but well worth it because of the quality of the locos seen there.

My thanks to photographers Christopher Campbell, Ian Spencer, Howard Forster, the late Frank Coulton, the late Eric Wilson, courtesy of Alan Brooks, the late Cecil Sanderson, the late George Watson, courtesy of Mrs Irene Watson and the late Walter Hodgson, courtesy of Eric Colling for allowing me to reproduce the images in this book, which I have thoroughly enjoyed doing. I must also give a very special thank you to Howard for doing the proof reading.

David Dunn Cramlington 2009

(*Cover*) **See Page 5**

(*Title Page*) **See Page 53**

Printed and bound by The Amadeus Press, Cleckheaton, West Yorkshire
First published in the United Kingdom by Book Law Publications, 382 Carlton Hill, Nottingham, NG4 1JA

Stanier 2-6-4T No.42428 stands gently brewing in the Maryport & Carlisle bay platform, at the head of a Barrow train on Sunday 5th October 1952. The locomotive is a Carnforth (11A) engine and has reached Carlisle on a regular working via the coast line – the long way round. In 1952 the magnificent screen of Citadel station was still in place but was looking rather worse for wear. *C.Campbell.*

3

Saturday, 8th September 1962, the right engine in the right place! Duchess No.46238 CITY OF CARLISLE stands in platform No.4 of Citadel station at the head of a southbound express. During most of the British Railways era this Pacific was an Upperby (Carlisle) engine and was usually kept in a good external condition. One of the two nameplates carried by the locomotive has been preserved in a museum in Carlisle, the other being in a private collection. A Stanier Class 5 stands in No.5 bay platform on a Leeds stopping train, via Settle. *C.Campbell.*

A lovely portrait of 8P Pacific No.46225 DUCHESS OF GLOUCESTER as it waits in the middle road of Citadel station, on Saturday 7th March 1964, to take over a southbound express. March 1964 and the forthcoming summer timetable was to be very much the swansong of the remaining 'Duchess' class Pacifics as they were summarily withdrawn six months later. At this time they were on stand by duties and often took over the duties of ailing diesels. However, southbound fish, meat and milk trains often had 'Duchess' haulage. Perth shed had a daily southbound 'perishables' working for a Stanier Pacific (someone else's of course) which took the engine as far as Crewe (and usually home). The external condition of the class during the final months of service was often deplorable and reflected the contempt of management to these magnificent locomotives. *F.Coulton.*

On the same Saturday, Stanier Class 5 No.44677, of Kingmoor shed, sets off north from Citadel past Viaduct goods yard on a parcels train. It is coupled to one of the self weighing tenders which was used to record accurate usage of fuel when a modification on this particular locomotive was being tested for its effectiveness. *F.Coulton.*

(*opposite*) In July 1952, Ivatt Cl.2 No.46457 of Workington shed stands in the M & C bay platform ready to depart on a Whitehaven train. Workington had an allocation of these lightweight 2-6-0s for the Penrith via Keswick services over a line which had a weak bridge. The Ivatt engines had replaced London & North Western 'Caulifower' 0-6-0s, which had worked the line in LMS days. In the background, a double-headed express, for the Midland line, hauled by a 'Jubilee' and Black 5, departs platform 4. *C.Campbell.*

Ready to leave Carlisle with a northbound express, Crewe North based 'Royal Scot' No.46158 THE LOYAL REGIMENT, stands at platform No.1 on Friday 14th April 1950 – next stop Glasgow (Central). At this time there were still a dozen or so Royal Scots in their original form, but all had been rebuilt with Diagram 102A taper boilers, and double chimneys, by 1955. No.46158 was dealt with over a rather prolonged (for Crewe works) 'General' overhaul which lasted virtually the whole summer of 1952, the engine finally emerging on 24th September, exactly four months after entry to the 'shops'. That was not the end of the story however. No.46158 had to re-enter the works a week later for rectification before working back to its home shed, which by then was Edge Hill. Shortly after this picture was recorded, this 'Scot' transferred to Holyhead for the summer season, then back to 5A before moving to Bushbury shed for an eight month stint prior to reallocating to 8A. *C.Campbell.*

Rebuilt 'Royal Scot' No.46136 THE BORDER REGIMENT sets off to Glasgow (Central) with a Down express on Saturday 8th September 1962. This 4-6-0 was an Upperby locomotive for most of the British Railways period and was generally kept in good external condition. However, it is looking a little woebegone here and the patch on the cabside, to the right of '7P', is where the bracket for the driver's name used to be located in balmier days when such pride in ones occupation was encouraged at all levels of management. On the date of this photograph No.46136 was apparently on loan to the North Eastern Region, its return to the LMR taking place on Sunday 9th but, this Crewe North working does not appear to support that fact. It transferred from 5A to Upperby week ending 15th September. Beyond the 'Scot', beneath the Victoria viaduct, lurks a BRCW Type 3 D53XX diesel on an Edinburgh train. *C.Campbell.*

Introduced in 1928 as a Post-Grouping continuation of Midland design, and too much Derby influence, 2P 4-4-0 No.40699 of Upperby shed, was one of a hundred and thirty-eight such engines built by the LMS at Crewe and Derby up to 1932. Our subject here was amongst the last of the 1932 Crewe batch. The 6ft 9ins coupled wheels enables the engine to appear to glide gracefully down to her home shed through platform 4 in August 1956, after having assisted a northbound express over Shap. Piloting heavy northbound expresses over the Cumbrian summit was typical work for the Upperby 2Ps but their somewhat spartan cabs would not be appreciated by crews during the winter months. This particular engine left Upperby in June 1957, firstly for Preston, then onto Patricroft, both sheds had the 4-4-0 for only short stays. Finally, in September 1958, No.40699 transferred to Llandudno Junction shed where it worked out its time until withdrawal in December of the following year. Much of its time at 6G was spent in store, a fate which most of the class suffered in their latter years. *C.J.B.Sanderson.*

It was rare to see two of the Ivatt Cl.2MT 2-6-0s working together so this is a somewhat unusual record of a pair of them. The date is Saturday 13th June 1964 and the nicely cleaned duo, Nos.46426 and 46458, both of Upperby shed, are passing Carlisle No.4 signal box, having just arrived at Citadel with the RCTS special THE SOLWAY RANGER. which they had hauled from Penrith via the Cockermouth, Keswick & Penrith line to Workington. Whilst the participants then took in the pleasures of Cumbrian industry past and present, aboard a six-car Derby lightweight d.m.u., the Ivatts, running tender first, returned the locomotive hauled stock to Penrith where the 2-6-0s then detached, ran round and coupled up to transfer the main train to Carlisle Citadel to await the arrival of the d.m.u.s. which had travelled along the coastal route from Workington. Their job done, the Ivatts departed Citadel whilst two veterans, Great North of Scotland 4-4-0 No.49 GORDON HIGHLANDER and Caledonian Railway 4-2-2 No.123, took the special onto Silloth. Return from Silloth to Citadel was also performed by the vintage Scottish pair and at Carlisle, the engine which had brought the train from Leeds earlier in the day, 'Merchant Navy' No.35012 UNITED STATES LINES, was waiting to take the special back to Leeds via the Settle & Carlisle. The southbound run over the S&C was apparently memorable too but that's another story. Meanwhile, our 2-6-0s settled down to the mundane after their short entry into the history books. The inevitable took place in 1966 and both engines when to the same scrapyard in Motherwell. Carlisle Cathedral tower peeps out behind the signal box. A nice retaining wall for the prospective modeller completes the scene. *I.Spencer.*

On a slightly overcast Saturday 29th July 1961 (what's new?) 'Patriot' No.45515 CAERNAVON heads a northbound extra at Citadel's platform 1. The train, 1S71, is possibly a Blackpool - Glasgow summer Saturdays Only train and the locomotive, based at Newton Heath, will be working through from Preston to Glasgow (Central). *C.Campbell.*

The fireman takes a well earned rest in his seat as 'Jubilee' No.45595 SOUTHERN RHODESIA stands at the north end of platform 1 at Citadel on Saturday 8th September 1962, having just arrived with a northbound express. Shortly after this picture was recorded, the 6P was detached from the train and pulled forward before getting ready to back down to Upperby shed for servicing. A similar engine took the train onwards to its final destination. One of only three 'Jubilees' to carry a plaque above the nameplate, No.45595 was a Crewe North locomotive at the time. *C.Campbell.*

Many mainline stations were remodelled by British Railways and Carlisle Citadel was no exception. Photographed under the overall roof while it was still intact, BR Standard 6MT Pacific No.72003 CLAN FRASER, heads a Glasgow (Central) – Manchester (Victoria) express in August 1956. The 'Clans' were highly unpopular with the Scottish footplate staff which probably assisted their early demise on that Region. Nos.72000 to 72004 spent most of their short lives allocated to Polmadie but in October 1957 Nos.72000, 72002, along with 72005 and 72006 from Kingmoor, were transferred to Haymarket to work on the ECML north and south of Edinburgh. The two Kingmoor engines returned to Carlisle during the following April whilst the Glasgow pair were sent back to 66A in June. Haymarket's crews did not like them and the 'Clans' were apparently failed for the slightest of reasons. However, BR tried again in November 1959 when all five of the Polmadie engines were transferred to St Margarets shed, with two of them later spending time at Haymarket. Nothing had changed and once again the BR Pacifics got the same reception, being failed for any minor fault. By April 1960 they were all back in Glasgow and Polmadie shed was stuck with them. Their unpopularity continued at 66A and all five spent time laid-up and 'stored' before they were finally, and prematurely, withdrawn. Incidentally, No.72003 was withdrawn while still carrying the early BR crest, possibly the only Pacific ever to do so. *H.Forster.*

An excellent top shot for modellers. Taken at Citadel on Thursday 23rd April 1964, this advantageous view shows all the upper surface detail on BR Standard 2-6-4T No.80113. The Hawick allocated engine stands ready to return home on the 6.13 p.m. stopping train. The Cl.4 tank arrived at the Waverley route depot, ex Great North of Scotland section, in December 1961 and worked from 64G until transferred to St Margarets shed in February 1966, and from where it was withdrawn during the following December. The photograph was captured from Victoria viaduct, which crosses the north end of Citadel station. *C.Campbell.*

With the ex L&NWR Crown Street goods depot dominating the background, former North British Railway and LNER C15 class No.67474 takes the empty stock of a Newcastle train out of Citadel's south end bay platform No.5, to release the train engine on an unknown date during the early 1950s. The view also shows the business end of Gresley brake 3rd, No.E16044. During the period when this scene was captured, this particular shunt was the preserve of one of Carlisle Canal's three C15s (67458, 67474, and 67481). After transfer to Eastfield shed in August 1954, this locomotive was fitted at Cowlairs works during the following month for push-pull working. It ended its days on the well known Arrochar - Craigendoran service on the West Highland line, a job that considerably lengthened its lifespan compared with its sisters it left behind in Carlisle; they were withdrawn in early 1956 whereas No.67474 worked through to early 1960, aged forty-seven. Just discernible on the right of the picture, are the remains of the former L&NWR signal box which controlled the south end of Citadel station until replaced by a modern box on the west side of the tracks. *E.Wilson.*

The humble yet ubiquitous LMS Class 3F 'Jinty' tanks also shunted the south end of Citadel station and for this, and other shunting jobs and trip working around Carlisle, Upperby maintained a fleet of about a dozen of the type. In September 1935, when the LMS was reorganising its motive power department and introducing a universal shed code, Upperby had ten of the type, Kingmoor none, whilst Durran Hill had three. After the latter depot closed later that year, its trio of 0-6-0Ts (7617, 7618 and 16639) were transferred to Upperby to make up the Bakers dozen, later rounded off to twelve, a number which remained virtually constant until withdrawals started in 1959. No.47667 was a late addition to the Upperby fleet, having been transferred from Camden in 1959. This engine was the first one of a batch of fifteen built in 1931 at Horwich (Nos.16750-16764) which also turned out to be the last of the type built for the LMS. The rather sedate scene here took place on Saturday 8th September 1962 as No.47667 gently idles away, waiting for its next turn of duty as station pilot. Another period feature of the photograph is the nice pile of parcels on the platform barrow awaiting delivery - history. *C.Campbell.* 17

(*opposite*) The last steam shunters at Citadel station were a group of Ivatt 2MT 2-6-2Ts which had been displaced from passenger duties by diesel railcars. Here we see overqualified, push and pull fitted, No.41222, which came from Leighton Buzzard, to spend its last two years at Upperby. Withdrawal came in December 1966 and it was dispatched for breaking to McWilliams, Shettleston and cut up by September 1967. *E.Wilson.*

A rare appearance of a splendid Gateshead V3, No.67645 in Citadel station during the summer of 1962. Despite their apparent suitability for the Newcastle - Carlisle line, the LNER V tanks rarely ventured west of Hexham in BR days. On my first visit to Carlisle, in the summer of 1956, I travelled behind V3 No.67653 of Blaydon shed, needless to say, it kept perfect time! *D.Dunn collection.*

This was something of an oddball. D49s were frequently seen at Carlisle on workings over the Waverley route by locomotives from either Canal shed or one of the Edinburgh area depots. D49/1 No.62731 SELKIRKSHIRE, fitted with a rebuilt Great Central tender, was a York based locomotive, running-in after a second Non-Classified visit to Gateshead works. What the 4-4-0 was doing at Carlisle on Monday 6th August 1956, is anyone's guess. Immediately above and behind the 4-4-0 is the original 1880-built northern end screen of the overall roof. The southern end screen, which was a mirror image of this one, lost much of its splendour some years earlier. *H.Forster.*

(*above*) Carlisle had always been a good centre for seeing double-headed passenger trains, mainly on services to and from the Glasgow & South Western route via Dumfries, and the Settle & Carlisle ex Midland line to Leeds. Pictured at Citadel on 17th July 1965, Standard Cl.5 No.73010 of Patricroft and 'Jubilee' No.45698 MARS of Bank Hall, had just arrived on a Glasgow (St Enoch) – Liverpool (Exchange) express. Lurking in the bay platform, possibly waiting to take a train south, is locally based 'Britannia' No.70003 JOHN BUNYAN, and in the centre road the dreaded Derby Lightweight d.m.u. *H.Forster.*

(*right*) No one could be called 'an anorak' in 1956! That item of clothing had not yet become popular by followers of MOTOR RACING – Yes, they were the first to adopt an anorak uniform. Young railway enthusiasts like Master Watson wore everyday clothing, which was often their school uniform plus the standard accessories, gas mask bag for sandwiches, and notebook. Just look at those sandals. Carlisle Citadel, 6th August 1956. *H.Forster.*

21

Recently ex-works, on 1st May 1963, from its final General overhaul, Kingmoor Cl.5 No.45481 runs light to her home depot past Viaduct (Caledonian) goods yard - which is still in full operation. The tracks in the far left background lead to Citadel station whilst those leading to the right, in the foreground, went to Dentonholme Joint Goods yard. *C.Campbell.*

On 14th January 1962, a long time Kingmoor engine shed resident, 4F 0-6-0 No.44009, heads a transfer coal train from Durran Hill to the then newly commissioned marshalling yard at Kingmoor. The train is passing through Bog Junction on the freight lines avoiding Citadel passenger station. To the right is Carlisle No.10 signal box and behind that can be seen the bridge carrying the former Maryport & Carlisle line into Citadel station, from which an Ivatt 2MT 2-6-0 can be seen reversing out. In the background can be seen the works of Cowans, Sheldon & Company Ltd, Crane Makers and Engineers. Cowans, Sheldon were responsible for supplying all four of Britain's pre-Nationalised railway companies, and many of their predecessors, with mobile breakdown and engineering cranes. BR carried on the trend. The lines curving off to the right, in the foreground, lead to Currock Jct. on the Maryport line. Immediately behind the photographer, at Rome Street Junction, a deviation took goods trains either (1) back onto the Glasgow line north of Citadel, at Caldew Junction, via Dentonholme Junction, or (2) off to Canal Junction where the lines to Edinburgh and Silloth diverged. This particular junction, or to be more correct the M&C chord, is all that survives in 2009. The original Joint Goods lines and Citadel deviation routes are all gone. Savour views such as this because they are pure history. *C.Campbell.*

Passing the former Caledonian Railway Viaduct goods yard in fine style, whilst heading a Euston-Perth express, on Saturday 8th September 1962, the magnificent and now preserved, 'Princess Royal' 8P No.46203 PRINCESS MARGARET ROSE departs from Carlisle in the evening sunlight. The Pacific had been specially cleaned by photographer Peter Robinson, albeit with the tender only half done but so what it still looks great! *C.Campbell.*

Turning the camera left through virtually 180 degrees, and going forward in time nearly two years, to Saturday 13th June 1964 we observe Ivatt 4MT 2-6-0 - 'Flying Pig' or 'Clodhopper' - No.43139 nearing Citadel station on the very last steam worked passenger train from Langholm Junction on the Waverly route. This locomotive spent its entire life at Carlisle, being allocated new to Canal (ex-NBR) shed, and ending her days at Kingmoor. Loyalty indeed, if such a thing was possible. *I.Spencer.*

Turning the clock back to Saturday 8th September 1962, and returning the camera to its original position, and owner, we view the event which took place shortly after No.46203 had sped north. The train itself is something less glamorous - a parcels train - but the motive power is worth a second glance. Kingmoor's newly acquired 'Jubilee' No.45738 SAMSON hurries north past Viaduct goods yard, destination Glasgow. This locomotive was a long time resident of Bushbury (Wolverhampton) shed, where it did much good work on the Euston - Birmingham expresses alongside sisters Nos.45733 to 45737 and 45741 and 45742, before being transferred north to Carlisle. The latter pair in the list, and No.34 too, came along to Carlisle with No.38, firstly to Upperby in November 1959 then to Kingmoor in July 1962. No.45738 was the first to be condemned, in December 1963. *C.Campbell.*

Four London, Tilbury & Southend 4-4-2T locomotives No's 41972, 41974, 41973 and 41971 slumber in what must have been seemingly perpetual store behind Carlisle's closed Durran Hill engine shed on 25th May 1952. Durran Hill was the most northerly outpost of the Midland Railway and in February 1936 the LMS decided to close the roundhouse because of duplicated locomotive facilities at Carlisle. However, during WWII the weight of freight traffic travelling through the city saw the LMS authorities authorize use of the coaling, watering and turning appliances at the depot, stabling was also undertaken but no engines were allocated. Although the shed was still nominally closed, locomotives arriving in Carlisle on freight trains during the BR era were also turned and serviced there. Back to our four tank locomotives which became surplus on the LT&SR by newer locomotives shortly after Nationalisation. They were then sent north to Scotland to find work at various sheds there (Dundee, Perth and Stirling in particular). However, after six months in the Scottish Region, where friends were hard to find, they all transferred – on paper - to Skipton but never actually got there, being put into store at Durran Hill whilst en route to Yorkshire. For the next three years they languished in Carlisle before finally being towed away to Derby, all coupled together, on 10th February 1955, by Kingmoor WD 2-10-0 No.90769. On arrival at Holbeck, the cavalcade was inspected and one of the 4-4-2Ts was found to have a hot-box. The WD was detached and worked home later whilst the 'Durran Hill four' eventually proceeded to Derby on the 16th and their fate in the works scrap yard. Many years after their escapade in Scotland, No.41971 managed to retain a 29A Perth (LMS) shed plate whilst No.41974 still had its 13D Shoeburyness plate attached. *C.J.B.Sanderson.*

On Sunday 25th May 1952 Cl. 5 No.44756 of Holbeck (Leeds) is shown at Durran Hill shed turned and serviced ready to work back home. The Stanier Class 5s eventually numbered 842 engines and many of the later locomotives were given experimental features in preparation for the introduction of the BR Standard classes. Holbeck shed was allocated five Class 5s equipped with Caprotti valve gear, and three of those were also fitted with double chimneys. All five frequently worked the Settle and Carlisle line. Still in its early BR unlined livery, No.44756 is lettered BRITISH RAILWAYS. The driver eyes' the photographer, nice cap! *C.J.B.Sanderson.*

(*below*) Sandwiched between two WDs on same day at the same shed, another Holbeck Caprotti Cl.5, albeit with a single chimney, was No.44753. It too was still in unlined black but with the early BR crest. The prominent steam pipes gave these locomotives a very distinctive look, and the valve gear made them free running engines. *C.J.B.Sanderson.*

As mentioned earlier, the former Midland engine shed at Durran Hill was closed as a depot in its own right by the L.M.S in 1936 but until it finally closed on 2nd November 1959, it was home to the LMS corridor tender (No.4999) which was used when locomotives were under test on the Settle & Carlisle line. BR also found it useful as a store shed for various engines (see also above). On 22nd July 1956, after the departure of the unfortunate LT&S tanks, former Lancashire & Yorkshire 'A' class 0-6-0 3F No.52418, of Workington shed, was languishing by the side of the roundhouse. How long the 0-6-0 had been 'stored' at this location is unknown and perhaps, more importantly, why was it dumped at Durran Hill when Workington shed had plenty of outside stabling room for a lone tender engine to rot away. Perhaps the coming of the diesel multiple units to Workington had some bearing on the matter? The 'A' class was finally withdrawn in January 1957 and cut up at Horwich works. Possibly because of weathering, it still clearly carried its large digit pre-1948 number 12418 on the cabside. *H.Forster.*

Duchess class 8P No.46229 DUCHESS OF HAMILTON, of Camden shed (1B), is ready to leave Upperby shed to take over the southbound *ROYAL SCOT* Glasgow (Central) – London (Euston) on 5th April 1958. In steam days, practices that had originated before the Grouping in 1923 still persisted into the 1950s. The *ROYAL SCOT* left Glasgow behind a Polmadie (Caledonian) based Duchess for Carlisle, and after 120 miles the Pacific was changed for a Camden (LNWR) Duchess, to run the remaining 300 miles to London. It would have been more logical to change locomotives at Preston, but it had always been done this way and continued so until steam traction was finally eliminated on the express working. *C.Campbell.*

A nice view taken from the footbridge at Upperby depot, with the edge of the roundhouse showing to the right and the primitive coaling stage (actually one of the first erected in the UK) to the left. The standby locomotive for mainline expresses at Upperby shed was always stationed in front of the Foreman's office; it is said that was because he wanted to see that the cleaners had done their job. Today, 7th March 1964, the standby engine is 8P No.46225 DUCHESS OF GLOUCESTER and the cleaners have completed their job, at least on the side facing the office. In the background is Cowans, Sheldon, the cranemakers, whilst at the bottom of the ramp leading from the depot, a lone railwayman can be seen going off duty. *F.Coulton.*

Another photograph taken outside the Upperby Foreman's office, this one on the 27th April 1964, shows one of the depot's own Pacifics, No.46250 CITY OF LICHFIELD looking resplendent in immaculate green livery. The cleaners had certainly earned their wages on this day. However, no matter how good the 'Coronation' appeared in this view, it was withdrawn six months later along with the remaining members of that magnificent class. On the hill behind is the enginemen's hostel which survives today as a hotel. Its modern outlines, compared to the more usual brick-built barracks found at certain other motive power depots, stems from the fact that when Upperby was rebuilt by BR in the early Fifties', a new 'barracks' was required to replace the ancient edifice built by the L&NWR. I wonder how many people tripped on the two wheelsets in the foreground, especially in the dark. One for the Health & Safety Inspector? *F.Coulton.*

Seven weeks before the previous photograph was recorded, on 7th March 1964, another green liveried albeit forlorn 'Duchess' No.46257 CITY OF SALFORD was in store at Upperby. The chimney is sacked, nameplates removed and the tender bereft of coal. The Engine History Card records the Pacific as being in store – serviceable - at Upperby from 30th December 1963 to 16th March 1964 – a seasonal trend for the Stanier Pacifics towards the end of their lives. This particular engine was the last Stanier Pacific to be built and, along with No.46256, was fitted with a modified rear truck and altered cab. It went into service after leaving Crewe works in British Railways livery. For the first ten years of its operational life, No.46257 was allocated to Camden depot but transferred to Upperby in September 1958. Withdrawn 12th September 1964, it was sold for scrap and cut up, along with seven others of its ilk, in a yard at Troon which was more akin to breaking up ocean going vessels. Behind the 'Duchess', on the left, we can see the curved concrete wall of the BR-built roundhouse whilst to the right is the repair shop. Upperby went through a long gestation period of rebuilding sheds and remodelling the yard under BR. The final stage of the work was not completed until 1958, just in time for the run-down of the steam locomotive fleet. The modern facilities did ensure a life after steam for some of the depot buildings and after the diesel fleet had finished with the place, the Engineering Department moved in with their mobile equipment. *F.Coulton.*

33

A rather pleasing study, captured on film at Upperby shed in October 1963, of Ivatt 2MT No.46455, showing detail of the tender cab whilst the 2-6-0 was queuing up to use the depot's coaling plant. This locomotive was allocated new to Penrith shed for working on the Keswick & Cockermouth line, for which these little 2-6-0s were ideal, working either chimney leading or tender first. When Penrith shed closed in June 1962, No.46455 was transferred to Upperby where she then spent the rest of her career. Upperby was actually graced with about eight of the Cl.2s towards the end of steam, one late arrival at the shed was a green liveried example from the Western Region, No.46513. The footbridge gave a very fine view of the shed yard and was a godsend for the young loco spotters of the day – every engine shed should have had one! *W.P.Hodgson.*

Both Carlisle Upperby and Leicester Midland motive power depots had new concrete roundhouses of the same design. The sheds, which were planned, and building work started by the London Midland & Scottish Railway, both had the turntable open to the elements so that smoke was easily dispersed. However, whereas the Leicester roundhouse was completed before Nationalisation, the Upperby shed was only just started when BR took over. Resident 'Duchess' No.46238 CITY OF CARLISLE, pictured in its home shed, was always kept clean by staff, as can be seen in this photograph recorded on 7th March 1964. The majority of the 'Coronations' were still in service at that time, and little did anyone suspect that the accountants were to act so ruthlessly a little over six months later, and withdraw the remainder of the class in one fell swoop on 25th September ??? 12th September surely according to EHC (46256 3rd October 64). This three-quarter rear view, looking up at the massive bulk of the engine, reminds many of us of the time when we used to 'bunk' the sheds with or without permits. To young 'spotters' trying to get all the numbers of the engines on shed, without getting caught, these gigantic locomotives certainly did look the part. *H.Forster.*

(*opposite*) Watched by a fireman on the 1st of August 1953, home-based Royal Scot class No.46165 THE RANGER (12th LONDON REGIMENT), is positioned in the Upperby roundhouse prior to going off shed. The concrete and glass walled roundhouse was built to replace a crumbling LNWR straight shed. The new shed had thirty-two roads, laid in the form of a complete circle, the 70ft. diameter articulated turntable was capable of accommodating a Stanier Pacific. *C.Campbell.*

7P 'Royal Scot' No.46155 THE LANCER, of Crewe North shed (5A) stands outside Upperby roundhouse on the 27th April 1964. The plate attached to the bufferbeam is to protect the Automatic Warning System train control equipment from a swinging front coupling. The AWS was a major safety improvement fitted from the late 1950s. It provided an automatic audible warning if a signal was passed at danger. It was fitted as a result of the 1952 Harrow disaster, where it is thought the crew of the London bound overnight sleeper train, which overran several signals at danger, because they had fallen asleep. *C.Campbell.*

A rather cold 27th April 1964 saw a warm but extremely filthy 7MT 'Britannia' Pacific No.70033 CHARLES DICKENS standing in Upperby shed yard awaiting its next turn of duty. By 1964 diesels were taking over the best of the passenger jobs and displaced passenger engines such as this one were doing parcels and fitted freight turns. They were regarded as 'common-users' and often were away from their home depots for weeks on end. Their external condition often became very poor and this is the case with No.70033. *C.Campbell.*

(*opposite*) A necessary, everyday job. A driver attends to the oiling of the motion of his Stanier Class 5, No.45449 of Wigan (Springs Branch) shed, in Upperby shed yard in July 1966. By this time it has had an economic paint job of plain, unlined, black livery. Ahead, in the queue for the coaling stage, is resident Ivatt Cl.2MT No.46458, its railtour days now well behind it. *E.Wilson.*

The famous railway photographer Canon. Eric Treacy once quoted in a book "You can't beat a Duchess for looks". Proof of this statement is this delightful study on the 7th March 1964 of a fabulous No.46225 DUCHESS OF GLOUCESTER, on standby at it home shed – Upperby (*see also page 31*). *F.Coulton.*

After having been coaled and watered, rebuilt 'Patriot' No.45523 BANGOR, of Camden depot, required turning before heading back to London on Sunday 6th August 1956. With the remodelling of the shed yard still being undertaken, the derelict building did not reflect the overall condition of Upperby depot, yet it still remained an eyesore, though not for much longer. *H.Forster.*

Ex-War Department 2-10-0 No.90763, a long time Kingmoor resident, was stored at Upperby shed after withdrawal, and in October 1963, just prior to removal to Darlington works for scrapping, it shares the 'dead' line with 'Princess Royal' No.46200. Approximately 1,000 locomotives were built in Britain during WWII to 'Austerity' design, using scarce materials and having no frills. Over 750 were purchased by British Railways after the war. Although built to minimum standards they proved remarkably durable. The larger of the two main types was a 2-10-0, with the locomotives purchased by BR allocated to the Scottish Region. As Kingmoor was part of the Scottish Region in early BR days, it was given an allocation of two or three WD 2-10-0s. All of the remainder of the class were withdrawn by a stroke of the pen in December 1962, whether or not they were in good condition. *W.P.Hodgson.*

'Royal Scot' No.46134 THE CHESHIRE REGIMENT, waits for the next assignment in Upperby shed yard on Sunday 17th June 1962. Newly acquired from Crewe North depot (three weeks previously), the 7P is both unkempt and streaked with lime, but it will not have another General or indeed any other overhaul as it was withdrawn during the following December. The 28th May transfer to Upperby was the engine's fourth residence at the shed and it was to prove to be its last and final move. Having enjoyed thirty-five years of hammering up and down the West Coast main line, and its important branches to Holyhead, Liverpool and Manchester, the engine managed to clock up two million revenue earning miles. By some quirk, only understood by those officials in the know, the engine never served north of the border, perhaps the regimental name precluding a stay of any length at Polmadie for instance. However, for its first eight years of life, the engine ran with the name ATLAS displayed. Now, surely that would be accepted anywhere. *G.Watson.*

A fine portrait of Ivatt 2MT No.46455 as she has her tender tank overfilled at Upperby in October 1963. The 2-6-0 was about to leave the depot to shunt the Crown Street goods yard. Notice the shed plate attached with an SC, denoting the engine was fitted with a self cleaning smokebox. *W.P.Hodgson.*

The interior of Carlisle Canal engine shed on Monday 5th May 1958, showing the rather curious track layout of: half roundhouse, half straight shed. The roundhouse was erected by the North British Railway and opened for business in 1862 as a pure (though square) roundhouse with twenty-four stalls. However, in 1910 the yard and the internal layout of the roundhouse was altered somewhat dramatically into the layout seen here. Two tracks were brought into the shed, along the full length of the north wall. Nearly half of the stalls radiating from the turntable were abolished and their pits filled in. Why such drastic measures were taken at Canal shed can only be speculated upon but one theory rests around the fact that certain important locomotives required for even more important Edinburgh bound expresses, were trapped in their stalls when the turntable failed, or some similar event took place. Not having too many roundhouse sheds on their system, the NBR must have fallen back on the straight road shed layout where every engine was accessible. Ex NBR Class N15 No.69215 has her boiler tubes attended to at the back of the shed whilst Class K3 No.61936 is worked on nearer the camera. Both locomotives are long term residents of Canal, the N15 working local trips and the K3 normally working the Waverley route. *C.J.B.Sanderson.*

Last of class. D31 No.62281 at Carlisle Canal in 1952. Built in 1884 and rebuilt in 1918, this doyen of the North British Railway outlived her sisters by nearly two years. Her original British Railways number was 62059, but she was renumbered in 1949 to make way for the new Peppercorn K1 class 2-6-0s, being built at that time. No.62059 and sister 62060 will always be remembered for their association with the Silloth branch. Dominating the background is the mechanical coaling plant supplied by the LNER. That such a shed should receive a mechanical appliance such as the coaler, when the likes of St Margarets, with its much larger allocation, made do with a manual coaling stage to the end, shows the one-time importance of this depot to the LNER. But there was more to come and in older to turn Gresley Pacifics a new and larger turntable was installed in the yard, just in time for the first allocations of A3s being received. However, all things must pass and it was certainly true in Carlisle Canal's case. The depot closed in June 1963 and was knocked down the following summer, all trace having disappeared some years since. *B.D.Nicholson collection.*

On Monday 25th February 1952, and still lettered L N E R, Class C15 No.67481 is pictured in the fifth year of British Railways ownership in Carlisle Canal shed yard, in the company of N15 No.69155 and an unidentified J39. It still carries typical North British features such as the Westinghouse pump and wingplates at the front of the smokebox. *C.J.B.Sanderson.*

(*opposite*) On the same day as the previous view, a favourite with Carlisle enthusiasts, Class J36 No.65216 BYNG, with its tender still lettered BRITISH RAILWAYS, stands in Canal shed yard. The locomotive was sent to France to help the Allied war effort during the First World War, and to commemorate this military service, each returning locomotive was named after an allied General or a Battle fought in the conflict. *C.J.B.Sanderson.*

(*opposite, bottom*) Carlisle Canal shed, although geographically situated in England, retained an allocation consisting mainly, for many years, of former North British Railway origin. The last N15 in the border city, No.69155 which had been used to shunt the former yards at NBR Canal Goods and the former North Eastern Railway London Road Goods, was pictured at Canal shed on 3rd June 1961. *H.Forster.*

Pictured at Canal shed on 3rd April 1961, N2 No.69564 was still retaining the GNR destination board brackets on its smokebox. The taller chimney was a characteristic of many Scottish members of the class. This engine had been sent down from Parkhead and was used on the Haltwhistle pick-up goods on a regular basis but was to be withdrawn two months after this photograph was taken. N2s were no strangers to Carlisle, the LNER had based some at London Road shed from 1930 to 1945, and from where they worked to Langholm and Haltwhistle. Standing in the background is Canal based B1 No.61290, showing the filled-in valances peculiar to all Scottish Region B1s. *H.Forster.* 49

(*opposite*) Having just been coaled, ex-North British 'Glen' class No.62484 GLEN LYON stands in Canal shed yard buffered up to a Gresley J39 in July 1961. This locomotive was allocated to Hawick at the time, albeit missing its shed plate, and was ending her days on local passenger workings to Carlisle. Built in 1913, this class did sterling work on the West Highland line between Glasgow and Fort William. *C.Campbell.*

Another ex-NBR class, the J35s worked hard on transfer freight and branch line work in the Carlisle area. On the 25th February 1952, J35 No.64478 is pictured in Canal shed yard taking a well earned rest. These engines spent a large amount of their time working tender first and to protect the crew from the elements, they were fitted with a tender cab. *C.J.B.Sanderson.*

(*opposite*) Carlisle Canal had four Gresley A3 Pacifics in their allocation. Their main use was for express passenger work over the Waverley route to Edinburgh, and the 2 p.m. passenger via North Wylam to Newcastle. Apart from visits to Doncaster works for overhaul, they were rarely seen elsewhere. On 5th April 1958, No.60093 CORONACH, which was a Carlisle engine during the whole of the BR steam era, is shown on Canal shed yard prior to returning to Doncaster 'Plant' works for rebuilding with a double chimney. *C.Campbell.*

Carlisle K3s did a tremendous amount of work, mainly over the Waverley route and on the Newcastle – Carlisle line. No.61858, fitted with a Great Northern tender which incidentally, has the crest around the wrong way, is pictured at Carlisle Canal on 3rd April 1961. The 2-6-0 was now at the end of its working life as it was withdrawn from service later that month. *H.Forster.*

On the second day of January 1959, 'Coronation' No.46227 DUCHESS OF DEVONSHIRE, of Polmadie depot, stands in Kingmoor shed yard being replenished with water, before moving off shed to return home to Glasgow on the Down *ROYAL SCOT*. A 'Jubilee' lurks in the background, and to the right of the locomotive are some of the large snowploughs usually attached to 4F 0-6-0s, to combat blizzard conditions on the many hilly routes in this part of the country. *C.Campbell.*

A very nice study of 'Clan' 6MT Pacific No.72008 CLAN MACLEOD in Kingmoor shed yard on Sunday 17th June 1962. Of the ten 'Clans' built - all in 1952 - Kingmoor received the second batch of five and kept them for most of their working lives. The first five went to Polmadie (Glasgow) but were not liked by the footplate men there. Just ten years after coming into traffic, the Polmadie 'Clans' were all withdrawn in December 1962. They were tried, and rejected, by the crews at Edinburgh's Haymarket and St Margarets sheds, but the Kingmoor lot soldiered on for a further three years until ousted by diesels. *G.Watson.*

55

Stanier 8F No.48175 in Kingmoor shed yard during October 1963. After the new Kingmoor marshalling yard was opened, the smaller yards at Upperby and Durran Hill were closed down. Thereafter, the role of transfer freights was ended and locomotives hauling freight through from the south worked into the new yard after which they all went to Kingmoor shed for servicing. This meant a very cosmopolitan array of locomotives could be seen on Kingmoor shed. Prior to the opening of the new yard, this 8F, from Mold Junction, would have been serviced at Upperby shed. The Thompson B1 in the background shows how varied the locomotives at Kingmoor had become. *W.P.Hodgson.*

Languishing between a Fowler 2-6-4T and a 'Jubilee', we see Stanier Class 5 No.45112, which spent much of its later life at Kingmoor, where it is pictured on the 7th March 1964. Although fully coaled up in the tender it is awaiting repair as the connecting rod is missing. A safety measure, after electrification in the Glasgow are, was the moving of the top lamp bracket away from its position in front of the chimney, to a new position half way down the smokebox door - which is very obvious in this photograph. Nearly thirty years old by now, the 4-6-0 had started its career at Edge Hill in April 1935. Two months later it transferred to Holyhead, a posting which lasted just over twelve years. Working its way back to England, the Cl.5 went to Llandudno Junction shed in July 1947 but moved on to Shrewsbury in early 1948 for a near four years residency after which it really 'pushed the boat out' and went north to Eastfield shed in Glasgow during November 1951. After a winter of working the West Highland line, No.45112 returned to England, just, during the following May for a seven year stay at Kingmoor. Loaned to Upperby during the early months of 1959, the Cl.5 returned to Kingmoor for another four years prior to a six-month transfer to Aintree. Finally returning in November 1963, No.45112 worked from Kingmoor shed until withdrawn in October 1966. *F.Coulton.*

A busy scene at the north end shed yard on 7th March 1964, highlights Stanier Cl.5 No.45437, of Agecroft shed, flanked by another Cl. 5 and a BR Standard class 9F 2-10-0. From 1964, when steam had a very short future, the lining on Stanier Class 5s was omitted as an economy measure as shown on this locomotive. *F.Coulton.*

(*opposite*) This was another 'last of class' veteran visiting Kingmoor for repairs. On Sunday 5th October 1952, and with the front coupled wheels missing, ex-Caledonian 4P Pacific tank No.55359, of Beattock shed, graces the yard with its considerable bulk. Never fitted with a smokebox numberplate, this engine was the last of a series which were built in 1917 for passenger work from Glasgow to the Clyde Coast. Displaced by Stanier and Ivatt 2-6-4Ts, they ended their days as bankers on the ascent to Beattock summit. *C.Campbell.*

Stanier Class 5 No.44727 has the blower in operation and drain cocks open, whilst ready to move off on 7th March 1964. Photographed on the east side of Kingmoor shed, next to the repair shops, this locomotive was allocated to Kingmoor for the whole of its working life and was another of the experimental series, being fitted with a steel firebox from new. It was withdrawn in October 1967, just eighteen years old. *F.Coulton.*

Kingmoor had a number of large snowploughs which were put to good use during severe winters. Here on the shed yard on 7th March 1964, we see an example fitted to Class 4F No.44457, which is in steam and ready to turn out at the drop of a snowflake. This size of plough was about the largest which could be fitted to a locomotive. The next size up was an independent snow plough which ran on its own wheels and was propelled in front of the pushing engines or engines. These particular ploughs were often constructed on old tender chassis and were often ballasted to give them an extra punch. Northern winters often lasted until the end of March and, on occasion, into April. Stanier 8F No.48321 stables on the left. *F.Coulton.*

After the closure of Carlisle Canal shed, ex-LNER locomotives working in from Edinburgh were serviced at Kingmoor and here, on 30th April 1964, we see Gresley A3 No.60100 SPEARMINT, of Haymarket shed, awaiting her return working. This particular engine was the steed of Norman McKillop who wrote under the pseudonym of Toram Beg in the Fifties railway press; I wonder what he would have thought of the Pacifics condition! The latter day 'improvements' to the locomotive are shown – German style smoke deflectors, AWS gear and the top lamp bracket moved to just above the number plate. *C.Campbell.*

This was a surprising visitor to Kingmoor but as the months of the transition period from steam to diesel went on, anything could and often did occur which was very much out of the ordinary – interesting times indeed. In December 1962, a long-time York resident Thompson A2/3 No.60524 HERRINGBONE, along with two others of the class (Nos.60512 and 60522), was transferred north to Scotland. The A2/3s were basically 'surplus to requirements' at York and had been stored at Scarborough shed for some months prior to transfer. St Margarets shed (60512, 60524) and Aberdeen Ferryhill (60522) were the first ports of call for the trio of Pacifics but in September 1963 they were all transferred to the former Caledonian and LMS depot at Polmadie, from where No.60524 had worked down to Kingmoor, where it was seen on 7th March 1964. At first, the A2/3s became regular visitors to Kingmoor but, like everything else associated with steam traction at that time, their non-standard presence at Polmadie created numerous problems regarding spares and the difficulty in securing such from workshops 'foreign' to the fitting staff at 66A. Inevitably they were laid up at the back of the Glasgow shed awaiting either transfer away or withdrawal. One managed to get away to Dundee whilst the other two were eventually condemned at 66A. *F.Coulton.*

A busy scene in October 1963 at Kingmoor shed yard featuring 'Clan' No.72009 CLAN STEWART, making a fair amount of smoke, a Class 5 on the same road, and a filthy Hughes/Fowler 'Crab' No.42791. The 2-6-0s, nicknamed 'Crabs' because their cylinders were inclined, were commonly seen at Kingmoor which had an allocation of approximately a dozen of this type for much of the BR era. In this case, however, No.42791 was a visitor from Gorton shed in Manchester. *W.P.Hodgson.*

Another rare visitor to Kingmoor was this BR Standard Cl.9F 2-10-0, No.92063 from Tyne Dock, which is pictured on the turntable in 1965. The Tyne Dock 9Fs were fitted with compressed air pumps for opening the doors on the iron ore wagons which they hauled to Consett steelworks. The ten-coupled engines rarely strayed from their Consett workings, but by 1965 some of their duties were being taken over by Type 2 diesels making many of the 9Fs surplus for the iron-ore trains. Thereafter, until either withdrawn or transferred away, they were used on normal freight workings. This view of the turntable at Kingmoor shows its position at the south end of the rather generously laid out yard. The West Coast main line passes alongside the depot affording a good view of the locomotives stabled outside the large shed. Today, like many former steam sheds, you would be hard pressed to find any traces of the establishment. *F.Coulton.*

This undated picture from the spring of 1965, shows Stanier and BR Standard Class 5 4-6-0s congregating at Kingmoor's turntable. The Standard 5, No.73007 was from Perth and would need to point north (to the right) to get home comfortably. On the other hand, Stanier 5 No.45106, was one of Kingmoor's own and could be going anywhere. Kingmoor motive power depot did become something of a pilgrimage destination for thousands of enthusiasts towards the end of steam, its army of 'Britannia' Pacifics being one draw, whilst the fact that this place became the most northerly operating steam shed in the country was another attraction. The fields in the background, beyond the WCML, and virtually opposite the steam shed (out of frame to the right), became the site where Carlisle diesel depot was eventually built. *F.Coulton.*

Miniature snowplough fitted and Kingmoor based Stanier Cl.5 No.45012 stands beside the repair shops on the east side of the shed building on Saturday 7th March 1964. A piston rod guide cover, and part of the front valance, lie on the footplate, and are probably the reason for repairs being undertaken. This was one of the earliest built class 5s dating from 1935 and featured a combined steam dome and top feed. Much of this locomotives life had been spent in Scotland or shedded close to the country. After initial acceptance at Crewe North from April to June 1935, it was sent to Inverness. In April 1939 Perth got it for three months before it went to Corkerhill in July. Shortly after the outbreak of war Inverness got it back in time for some hard work during the period of hostilities. In November 1947 Motherwell became its home but it returned to 60A in June 1950. Crossing the border for probably the first time in nearly eighteen years, No.45012 was reallocated to Kingmoor in September 1952 for a ten year spell. Wanting to explore further the strange country from which it originated, the Cl.5 ventured across Carlisle to Upperby shed in March 1962 but returned to Kingmoor fifteen months later. In April 1966, at the grand old age of thirty-one, No.45012 transferred to Barrow where it worked until condemned during the following October. *F.Coulton.* 67

The interior of the repair shop roads on the east side of Kingmoor shed in October 1963. In the twilight of its career an unidentified 'Royal Scot' 4-6-0 is stripped of its left-hand side motion. It is nameless and was probably already relegated to freight service. In the background receiving attention are pair of 'Britannia' Pacifics, Nos.70036 BOADICEA and 70041 SIR JOHN MOORE, plus another 'Royal Scot'. The identity of the 'Scot' will remain a mystery because a least a dozen of the class were associated with Kingmoor during the time of the photograph: 46110, 46115, 46128, 46132, 46150, 46157, 46160, 46162, and 46166 actually allocated to Kingmoor whilst 46118, 46136 and 46141 were allocated to Upperby. Of course there were still more than a dozen still active on the WCML, but resident at other sheds, during this same period. So, in conclusion, it could have been any 'Scot' still active on BR, except those at Annesley, but there again… *W.P.Hodgson.*

Another interesting and informative view inside the Kingmoor repair shop on that same day in October 1963. This one shows 'Britannia' No.70041 SIR JOHN MORE having repairs to its motion, note the connecting rod on the floor. Behind is a Stanier Cl.5 4-6-0 and on the left is another Kingmoor 'Brit', No.70036 BOADICEA. Both 'Britannias' started life as top link motive power at Stratford shed, working expresses on the Great Eastern lines out of Liverpool Street, but their current condition belies their relegation to mundane mixed traffic work. Note that both still had their nameplates attached at this time. *W.P.Hodgson.*

(*opposite*) Another photograph from October 1963 reminds us just what hard and thoroughly unpleasant work it was to service steam locomotives as an unidentified Stanier Cl.5 has the ash and char cleaned out of the smokebox. If this particular task was not carried out on a very regular basis, the accumulated ash would effectively block the smokebox and seriously affect the steaming of the locomotive. The cleaner we see here is wearing safety goggles (quite an advance for 1963) but what about dust mask. Well '…one thing at a time…' as they say. *W.P.Hodgson.*

The first diesels to make serious inroads into the main line passenger working on the London Midland Region were the English Electric Type 4 1-Co-Co-1 2000 h.p. diesel-electrics. They were robust machines and long-lived but a number of failures occurred on the road, often as a result of the inexperience of the men driving them. Here on, Sunday 17th June 1962, we see D216 CAMPANIA at Upperby, its home shed, awaiting the next turn of duty. The diesels allocation plate is mounted just below the number. The early examples of the class had electric lighting but also carried the white discs on the nose at each end, as these headcodes were still used on the Great Eastern section on which some of them worked. Later examples had a split two box headcode whilst models turned out later had the full box in the centre of the nose, displaying a four-character code or train number. For example '1S24' meant an express passenger train terminating in the Scottish Region. D216 never had either type of code boxes and except for a change of livery to blue in later life, carried on much as it was in this view at 12B during the age of steam. *G.Watson.*

Men at work! The date is unknown but it could have been virtually any time from 1935 to 1968. A Stanier Cl.5 (Kingmoor did have a lot of them) stands next to the depot's coaling plant, waiting for the fitters to decide how to execute a repair. "Any ideas?" "I haven't a clue, but I've got a big hammer!", replies his mate. "Go and make a cuppa and leave the hard work to me". It looks like a new connecting rod has been fitted so let us hope it was of the right type. *W.P.Hodgson.*